Sometimes Words Are Enough

E.T. Dang

BookLeaf Publishing
India | USA | UK

Presentation by *BookLeaf Publishing*

Web: www.bookleafpub.com

E-mail: info@bookleafpub.com

ISBN: 9789357448949

First edition 2022

DEDICATION

To everyone that wakes up each day and decides to keep going

ACKNOWLEDGEMENT

To the best friend who encouraged me to seek out a passion for words

PREFACE

This is my first hand at being vulnerable on a page that will possibly be seen by others. I know not all will find value in my words but I hope that it somehow finds at least one person.

To My Cloud

I feel light as a cloud and jubilant as a bee near
milkweed
But when I see your face it's like looking right at
the sun
Painful and blinding

When it starts to sting a cloud appears
Suddenly the pricks subside and shade calms the
bite
I hold myself still and ground my roots into the
hard clay

I remember that the burn is just temporary
The sun will always flash but I will keep
growing
My roots spread through the clay and when I
cannot hold myself

I will always have the clouds

Metamorphic Rock

Talking to you singed like swallowing hot sand
I tried my hardest to block the sand before it
could burn
But I was never fast enough
The sand built up in crevices scorched into my
throat
Where tears and anger slowly mixed with the
grains
Under the pressure I became hardened

Eventually you ran out of sand but it was too
late

Alert

I thought your halo grew red
from the love I poured into you
But they were red sirens and flags
Forewarning me of the storm

Death of the Mouse

We have been competing as cat and mouse for so long that I have forgotten this began as a game. I thought I was the cat but soon became your prey. You hold me long enough to hope the game is finally over but a claw appears to claim its reward. I keep asking myself when I will stop playing this game with you.

It is when I have run out of space for you to score.

Dimmed Light

I watched you go from a burning star
with so much light and warmth
to a cloud of ashen dust
when you crashed into his orbit

Misshapen Rose

"Contrary to popular belief a perfect rose is easy
to grow
All you need is a lot of sun" echoed in my head
So I reached and bent for any light I could
But I grew crooked and warped
So you moved on to other roses

Fractured

I held my cup with trembling fingers
Contorting my limbs to reach your ever moving
glass
Twisted and deteriorating I never let your glass
empty

The slightest smile in my direction warmed my
frostbitten fingers
Your laugh buzzed in my head as I ran for more
water
My joints oiled with temporary affection that
eased the ache

But none of it ever lasted
Water was dripping from my fingertips
Until my grip grew brittle and ultimately my
glass slumped to the ground

A hairline crack in the base of my cup appeared
I could now only fill your glass half as fast
So you went to other hands

Even when you left the glass behind I wanted to
keep pouring

A Memory

You are perfect, for someone else
Were words that made me ache
Because they used to be
You are perfect, just for me

Open

Vulnerability is not a weakness as much as the world wants you to think it is. It is for yourself and not others. So no matter the direction, you can always say you were honest. Even if they weren't.

I Will Be Your Shoulder

On days where you cannot gather yourself to get
up
Remember that your brilliance is not so easily
smothered
Even a flame can reignite from its wisps
And if you cannot start alone then I will lend
you my light

Note to Self

Happiness is feeling long searched and sought
after
But I realized it is a feeling created
When you nurture the happiness you seek within
yourself
You no longer pine for it from others

I Learned to Live With the Cold

Our souls didn't run into each other by accident
They were destined to collide and crash
Because the moment we met
my world tilted a little further on its axis
But I failed to realize that our souls weren't
meant to
Meld together forever but only for a short
instance
When you peeled away from me
I felt the cold creep in where your spot used to
be

To Her

I'm sorry that I could not be a better friend

I was a fish drowning in water who couldn't
speak up
Because how could I not bare to live
In the environment I was made for

Everyday I wished to see myself floating belly
up
So I swallowed rocks to keep me settled
But soon the rocks pulled me down
Hurting you in the process

So please know that

I hope you get all the things you've ever wanted
Till your rib cage is over flowing with joy and
love
And if you ever return to me I'll be a better
friend

Where is Home?

You can move to new states
Live in different cities
But if you never find the comfort
that you seek within yourself
Nowhere will ever be home

Life Cycle of a Bruise

Pink
The color of your sweet words
Red
The color of rage in your voice
Purple
The color of settled swollen skin
Blue
The color of loneliness
Black
The color of defeat
White
The color of hope

When You Meet Unconditional Love

The kindest love I've ever known has come
from her
I will not try to to describe the feeling of being
aligned so perfectly
That you can't remember how you lived
unbalanced for so long

You're Doing Your Best and That's Enough

I have made it to this point
Past the places I thought I would never leave
But here I stand a little bruised but still strong
Finally able to breathe

Not the End

Please never forget that you are talented and
wonderful
When life has been hard you have not given up
Each wave that has tried to consume you has not
won
I know some waves were harder to tread than
others
But you are still here and that is something to be
so proud of yourself for

www.ingramcontent.com/pod-product-compliance
Lightning Source LLC
LaVergne TN
LVHW050303200726
843509LV00015B/3126